The Student's Guide to Exam Success

How to get great grades with less studying

Andrew K. J. Tan

Aktive Learning
10 Anson Road #21-02
International Plaza
Singapore 079903

E-mail: publisher@aktive.com.sg
Online book store: http://www.aktive.com.sg

ISBN 978-981-08-2860-8

National Library Board Singapore Cataloguing in Publication Data

Tan, Andrew K. J., 1980-
    The student's guide to exam success : how to get great grades with
less studying / Andrew K.J. Tan – Singapore : Aktive Learning, c2009.
    p. cm.
    ISBN-13 : 978-981-08-2860-8 (pbk.)

    1. Test-taking skills. 2. Examinations – Study guides. 3. Study
skills. I. Title.

LB3060.57
371.26 -- dc22   OCN318304196

Printed in Singapore

Dedicated to my dearest wife

Contents

Introduction

As a student you cannot avoid taking tests, and how you do on those tests will have a dramatic impact on the rest of your life. It affects what schools you get into; how parents, teachers and peers perceive you; what scholarship and career options are open to you; even how much you enjoy school and your level of self-esteem.

I have excelled at taking exams. This has helped me get into top schools and even win a scholarship to Stanford University. And I managed to do this while living a mostly balanced life with time for friends and extracurricular activities.

But with only above-average intelligence at best and a fair dose of laziness, the credit has to go to my skill at test-taking. I have seen how this skill has opened doors and given me many opportunities. I have also seen other students struggle with exams, and how demoralised and stressed they felt. These were intelligent, hardworking students who knew a lot more than me, but simply had poor test-taking skills.

I wrote this book because I believe what I have to share will have a major impact on your life. Almost any student can improve their grades if they put some effort into polishing their test-taking skills. Even if you are a top student, I believe this book will help you achieve similar results while studying less, giving you more time to play and enjoy life.

You don't go to school to take exams. You go to school to get an education. Being good at taking exams will help you get into the best schools and get a good education. It will also free up time so you can study less and spend more time on your hobbies or hang out with friends, both of which will probably turn out to be more important to the future quality of your life than what you learnt in the classroom.

There are many myths about test-taking, and about what it takes to excel at exams. Let's explore two of these:

Myth #1: Smart students always do well in exams

Intelligence does not automatically lead to good grades. I have known many intelligent people who did poorly in school. Perhaps they had not studied for the test, or had no interest in the subject, or did not fit well into the school system.

Even geniuses can do poorly in school. When Albert Einstein, winner of the Nobel Prize in Physics and creator of the Theory of Relativity, was a teenager in a German secondary school, he bickered with teachers and resented the school's regimentation. He felt the educators were too restrictive and focused on rote learning, hindering his creativity and individuality. He also failed an entrance exam into a Swiss university.

> *"To me the worst thing seems to be a school principally to work with methods of fear, force and artificial authority. Such treatment destroys the sound sentiments, the sincerity and the self-confidence of pupils and produces a subservient subject."*
> — *Albert Einstein*

To do well in an exam, any student, regardless of his intelligence, needs to apply himself to learn the curriculum material, then effectively demonstrate his knowledge during a test. It is true that an intelligent student can learn things faster if he applies himself correctly, but he still needs to study and have good test-taking skills.

Myth #2: Hardworking students always do well in exams

Effort does not automatically lead to good grades. You can study all day but learn nothing. Maybe you had poor study skills or were studying the wrong material. You can even study all day and learn everything but still do poorly in tests. Maybe you made a lot of careless mistakes or you panicked and blanked out.

The point is that learning and testing are two different things. Think of the difference between learning and testing as the different between jogging and doing a hundred-meter sprint. In the former you are relaxed and working out for your health; in the latter you are taking part in an intense and stressful event. To do well in exams you need a combination of optimal learning and superior test-taking.

Optimal learning depends on good study skills and putting in effort to make the material stick. Superior test-taking focuses solely on the skills involved in the run-up to and during the exam itself. It has very little to do with learning.

Exam skills help you get better grades regardless of how much you studied. For example, assume two people have the same knowledge about a particular subject. Everything else being equal, the person with superior exam skills will do better.

Being good at taking tests will save you a lot of stress and anxiety. It will also help you become more successful in school and in life. To ace an exam, you need both good study skills and test-taking skills. I will touch a bit on the former but this book will focus on the latter.

My test-taking strategy was developed and honed over the years as I learnt how to play the game. I was driven by my laziness. I wanted to put in the minimum effort to get great (not necessarily perfect) grades.

My test-taking strategy is based on both *principles* (general guidelines or "truths" to prep yourself psychologically) and *techniques* (concrete things to do). My method is general enough to work for most people, but there certainly are other methods that could work just as well. You have to try it, tweak it based on what works for you, and make it your own.

There is much more to life than taking tests. I will be happy if what I share helps you get an A or a 95% score. But what I really want (and the motivation behind my writing this book) is for you to enjoy all that life has to offer, and not spend all your time trying to "fix" this part of your life, constantly pressured by your parents or teachers.

Put in a reasonable amount of time and effort to study, take the exam like a maestro, and perform splendidly in school. Then go hang out with your friends, play sports, read good books or brighten up someone else's life.

Chapter Summary

✎ To do well in an exam you need to first learn the material then be able to demonstrate your knowledge during a test

✎ Superior exam skills help you get better grades regardless of how much you studied

Part One:
Secrets of the Successful Student

Brief Contents

Why You Have To Take Tests

Why do you have to take tests in the first place? The people who want you to do so usually have the following motives:

To find out how much you know

If they could stick a probe into your brain or read your mind to find out how much you know, they would. But they can't. So the next best way to quantify this is to test you. The score you get is an indicator of your knowledge. This score may not accurately reflect your true understanding of a subject, but it will be used as it is the most convenient measure.

To track your learning

Let's take a high level view of your education. Your learning follows a curriculum, a group of subjects you are supposed to study. Each subject will have a sequence of topics or learning objectives, which contains the details of what you are supposed to know.

For example, lower level mathematics could have topics such as addition, subtraction, multiplication and division, while higher level mathematics would include more complex topics such as geometry and calculus. You can get a good sense of what you're supposed to learn by looking at the contents page of your textbook. Tests are given to you along the way to track your progress and to measure how competent you are in the subject matter.

To compare you with others

We live in a relative world. How do educators determine whether you are ahead or behind the curve? They look at how you fare versus your peers. They want to determine whether you are average, below average, or above average.

To determine your educational path

At the highest level, the education system needs to prepare and add value to the human capital of a country to meet its needs. You are part of that human capital – your education, experience and abilities have an economic value. There's no need to feel like a cog in a machine – you are also an individual with unique talents, and I hope your teachers, parents and friends see that.

But every country needs to have its factory workers, civil servants, doctors, lawyers, engineers, bankers and so on. And there are limited resources and limited places in the universities, polytechnics, and other institutes of higher learning. Most people wouldn't mind being a lawyer or banker and making lots of money. But how does a country (via its education system and employers) allocate its human resources in the most optimal way? To a large extent this is determined by your test scores.

Chapter Summary

You have to take tests to help educators:

✎ Find out how much you know

✎ Track your learning

✎ Compare you with others

✎ Determine your educational path

Why Tests Are Important

Tests are important because test scores are important. Your scores signal not just how much you know, but also the quality and potential of your human capital.

Doing well in tests gives you more choices

If educators believe you have high potential, they are likely to allocate more resources to you and give you more opportunities. You not only get a better education but also more choices in life. You can *choose* what you want to do in life and not be forced into something you dislike. Having the luxury of different options is a very valuable thing.

> *"Exams are a necessary but unfortunate inconvenience of your schooling experience. They are meant to test your understanding of the subject matter, to give educators a way to judge how well you know your stuff, and as a prod to motivate you to study."*
> — *The Student's Guide to Life*

Doing well in school and getting a good education will protect your financial future. As a country develops, it needs more highly skilled workers. The economy moves from being based on farms and factories to one based on labs and lots of people sitting in front of computers.

This is known as the knowledge economy, where value is created not by assembling things together faster but by being able to use your brain to solve new problems and exploit opportunities. This is where the world is moving, and if you are well educated and adaptable, you will be in greater demand and people will pay you more for your efforts.

I know this sounds so serious and feels foreign to your immediate problem of having to pass that test next week, but only by seeing the big picture can you understand why it is important and why you should even bother studying for it.

Tests motivate you to study

On another level, tests are also important because they are both a prod to get you to organize your material and study it, and also a way for you to benchmark how much you are really learning. I know the best way to get me to study is to have an exam on it next week!

Hopefully we can learn things because we find them fun or interesting (i.e. intrinsic motivation), but sometimes the threat of a looming exam is the jolt we need to put nose to textbook and start studying (i.e. extrinsic motivation). Learning is an effortful process, we are lazy bums, and so a test is sometimes needed to bridge the two.

Chapter Summary

Tests are important because:

- ✎ Doing well in tests gives you more choices
- ✎ Tests motivates you to study

The Mindset Of A Successful Student

Successful students know minimal studying doesn't mean no studying. They know meaty subjects still need a lot of effort and preparation to digest properly. What successful students look for is the most *efficient* way to score good grades on any test.

The Pareto Principle

Successful students who do not want to spend all their time studying know they have to score high points but not full points. When they prepare for exams, they aim to get a good grade, not 100%.

Why? Because the first 80% of points on the average test are fairly easy to get if you prepare adequately, but the next 20% are much tougher. The difficult questions in a test usually require much more brain power and effort to answer, take more time, and deal with more complex material. If you want to score 100%, you not only need to know *everything* that has been taught in class (perhaps even more), but also need to make *zero* careless mistakes.

The smart students would rather spend less effort studying and still get most of the marks in a test than to put in many more times the effort to get a few extra points. How much effort can be saved?

13

Vilfredo Pareto (1848-1923) was a French-Italian economist who observed that 80% of the income in Italy went to 20% of the population. He carried out surveys in other countries and found to his surprise that a similar distribution applied. Later this generalized principle – that for many events, 80% of the effects come from 20% of the causes – became known as the Pareto Principle or the 80/20 rule.

As it applies to tests, if you imagine that 100% of the points on a test require a 100% effort from you, 80% of those points could have been obtained by putting in just 20% of that effort. Sounds like a smart thing to do, doesn't it?

I'm not saying that you should only aim for 80%. When you prepare for a test (and have sufficient time to do so) you should prepare to score 100% of the marks, but not be obsessed by it. You should try and cover all the material that will be tested (not necessarily all of what has been taught in class), but you are not consumed by knowing *everything*.

Being a perfectionist takes a lot of time and effort, and almost always lead to disappointment. Why be so hard on yourself? It is good enough to do well.

The power of focus

The subtitle of this book is "How to Get Great Grades with Less Studying". How do you do that? In one word: *focus*.

When studying for an exam, successful students are able to concentrate on the material. They attack it with as much accuracy as a ninja throws a shuriken star. So, for example, studying in a group may not be conducive to focus as there are many opportunities to get distracted.

When taking exams, successful students are able to completely focus on the question at hand and devote their mental energy to answering it. This minimizes the careless mistakes they make.

At the same time they have a sense of urgency when they tackle the test, and are aware of the limited time they have. The mindset they adopt is something I call "hurried cautiousness" – the state of being fast yet careful.

Focus Like A Ninja

Treat it like a game

Do you know people who never get stressed when exams are around the corner, don't seem to study much, yet often end up near the top of the class? Okay maybe they're just geniuses (in addition to being very annoying), but thankfully there aren't too many of them around.

More likely these are students who just think differently about exams. They treat it like a game, a game which has rules they can figure out. These students come up with a strategy to play this game and then practise it, getting better and better at taking tests until after a while it seems almost effortless (to you, that is). That's what experts do – whether in sports or music or taking exams – they make it look so easy.

Treat exams like a game. Once you know the rules, have a strategy and practise it for a while, you can win on a regular basis. The rest of this book will help you figure out the rules and develop a strategy that works for you.

Mind like water

Yes, some tests are more important than others, but a single test is not a life and death issue – more important is how you do over a period of time. Successful students do not obsess about how they do on one test. They know there is more to life than a test, and they are far more than a grade on a piece of paper. Thinking this way will help you reduce test anxiety and stress, helping you perform at an optimal level.

Successful students go into a test confident and with a

calm and peaceful state of mind. They have a mind like water, ready to deal with anything that might come up. Imagine a pool of undisturbed water – it is perfectly still and calm. Drop a stone in it and the water ripples as it deals with the impact of the stone, but then quickly returns to its placid state, as though nothing happened. I learnt the phrase "mind like water" from productivity guru David Allen's book *Getting Things Done*, which I highly recommend.

Successful students are calm and confident because they are well-prepared. They know that as long as a question on the prescribed syllabus comes out, they will be able to answer it. They are ready for anything.

Mind Like Water

Minimum effort, maximum results

Your time and energy is limited. You have to choose how you spend it to achieve your goals. You will always have too many things to do and too little time to do them. If you want to have more time to do the things you like (e.g. play), you have to do the things you don't like (e.g. study) in less time. In other words, you have to learn to be more *efficient*, spending less time and effort to achieve the same or better results.

On a daily basis, you can minimize study time by making the most of class time. Pay attention and learn as much as you can in class. If you do not understand the concepts being introduced, clarify your doubts immediately. Take good notes in class to help you organize and keep track of your learning.

Do homework as quickly as possible while the material is still fresh in your mind. When I was in school I had a classmate who would start doing homework right after class (sometimes even during class!). He also used breaks or spare time between classes and would finish his homework within an hour after school ended. If he didn't know how to do it, he would seek the teacher's help right away. Imagine never having to bring any homework home!

Chapter Summary

✎ Spend enough time preparing for an exam to get a great grade, but don't obsess with being perfect (remember the 80/20 rule)

✎ Learn how to focus

✎ Treat the exam like a game – figure out the rules and the strategy to play

✎ Have a mind like water – take tests feeling calm and confident

✎ Learn as much as you can in class to minimize study time

The Skill Set Of A Successful Student

Studying versus training

There is a difference between studying to learn something and training to score in an exam. When you study to learn something, you spend time understanding the concepts and getting a clear sense of the big picture. Then you drill down to the details to "fill in" the holes in your knowledge. Outside of the exam periods, this is what you should be doing to get a good education, and the knowledge you've picked up will certainly help you during an exam.

However, if your goal is just to do well in a test and you are pressed for time, then your method of preparation will be different. You will be skimming the study material for the key concepts, and most crucially, you will be preparing by *answering questions*. In the most extreme case where the exam is tomorrow and you have not studied at all, you should skip the textbook and just work on the mock exams or practice questions.

Why do this? When athletes train for an event they practise the precise movements of their sport over and over again. They go through the motions repeatedly, building not only strength and speed but also training their muscle memory so that by the time the competition comes around, their actions are automatic.

Train for an exam by answering questions

What is it you actually do when you take an exam? You answer questions. That is what you should be practising. You can read through the entire textbook and memorize everything in it, but still be stumped when you take the test if you do not know how to answer the question. You can ace a test without opening your textbook by practising answering questions and learning the answers to those questions (although this is not recommended).

The well-prepared student will set aside sufficient time to study the material and understand the concepts, but he will go through it with questions in mind so that his study is directed. Then closer to the exam, he will focus on going through all the practice questions and tests he can lay his hands on, and training for it by doing exactly what he will be doing during the test itself – answering questions.

Why can't you just do the answering questions part and skip the whole studying part? Well you can if you're really desperate, but the smart students who think long-term don't do it because: 1) They actually want to learn something and gain knowledge 2) Being well-prepared is the best way to develop confidence on the test.

Chapter Summary

✎ Prepare for an exam by practising answering questions

Build Your Exam Muscles

The Rituals Of A Successful Student

No, I'm not talking about joining a cult. To put themselves in the right frame of mind to take the exam, successful students develop a personal routine in the period leading up to it.

Prepare spares

Prepare a packing list for the stationery you need during the exam, and include spares for everything. That means spare pencils, pens, rulers, erasers, and even a screwdriver and spare battery if you need a calculator (or just a spare calculator).

Preparing all your equipment will help you relax and feel ready for anything that might happen during the exam. Believe in Murphy's Law: anything bad that can happen will happen. Your pencil breaks, pen runs out of ink, calculator goes *kaput*. These things happen. And if it happens and you are not prepared with spare equipment you will panic and waste valuable time trying to get a replacement, which will affect how you do on the test. If instead you have prepared backups you will just shrug, take out your spare, and continue with the test (this has happened to me a number of times).

Pack your supplies the night before the exam

The night before the exam, pack stationery you need and food to eat. There were times I had to take two or even three three-hour long exams in a single day and I would pack bananas (a fantastic brain food), some chocolate bars, and a bottle of water into my backpack the night before. This not only gave me energy to think but also minimized the time wasted buying these things on the day itself so I could do some last minute review or just chill before the next exam.

The successful student is ready for any challenge, mental or physical. He studies the subject material and practises answering questions to prepare for the mental challenge, and he readies his equipment and food to meet any physical challenges during the exam. He is not afraid because he is prepared.

Chapter Summary

✎ Prepare a packing list for stationery (including spares and food)

✎ Pack your supplies the night before the exam

How To Maximize Your Grade While Minimizing Careless Mistakes

Human beings are imperfect and we make mistakes – accept it. This truth applies to every area of your life, but let's focus on test-taking for now. No matter how many times you check your work you will inevitably let a mistake or two slip by – perhaps you didn't see the word "not" in a question (which reverses the meaning); perhaps you solved the problem correctly but circled the wrong answer. It's ok. Successful students do not obsess about being perfect. Perfection is for robots; great is good enough.

Just as they have a ritual to prepare for exams, successful students also have a ritual when they take exams to maximize their grade and minimize careless mistakes.

Manage your time carefully

If there is one core skill of successful students, this is it: they plan and keep track of their time during an exam. Once the teacher says "you may begin", they don't rush to start the first question like everyone else, but instead flip through the paper to gauge how many sections and questions there are. They make a mental note of how much time they have on average for each question, and compose a strategy to tackle it. If information on the structure of the exam is available beforehand, they do this before taking the exam.

For example, if the exam is one hour long and there are twelve questions in it, you know you have five minutes to answer each question on average. If you have spent five minutes on one question and are going nowhere, move on. If you are only halfway through, spend another minute to wrap it up quickly and then move on to the next question.

Failure to manage your time properly is one of the commonest and saddest ways to do poorly in an exam. It is sad because you perform poorly despite studying hard and knowing the answers to the questions.

I have known too many people who have failed exams not because they did not study, but because they got stuck on one question and spent all their time trying to answer it, leaving a large portion of the exam blank as they ran out of time.

I cannot stress enough the importance of managing your time carefully. I recommend bringing a watch you can take off and put in front of you to help you keep track of time. Always plan your time and stick to your plan. It is okay to skip a question or two if it is going to suck up too much time. Your preparation efforts and exam skills will ensure you get enough points in the rest of the test to do well.

Attempt every question

Unless you are penalized for wrong answers (i.e. have points subtracted), you should attempt every single question, even if you have to guess. If a multiple choice question stumps you just circle the choice that makes the most sense or *feels* right. If it is a structured response question write down something you know even if you are not sure of its relevance. If it is a mathematics question write down a formula. If it is an essay question and you have run out of time jot your answer down in point form.

These are all opportunities for you to score additional points even if you know nothing. Do not leave any blanks. Do not underestimate the power of partial credit (otherwise know as "mercy marks" or "pity points"). If you're stuck, don't stress, just guess!

Read the question carefully

You can only score points in a question if you answered the question correctly. Many students read quickly through a question and misunderstand what is being asked. They then waste time giving a comprehensive answer to the wrong question.

For example, take a look at this question:

Mammals are an animal of the class Mammalia, characterized by being warm-blooded, having hair and feeding milk to its young. Except for the five species of monotremes (which lay eggs), all mammals give birth to live young. Most mammals also possess specialized

> *teeth, and the largest group of mammals, the placentals, uses a placenta during gestation. The mammalian brain regulates endothermic and circulatory systems, including a four-chambered heart. Which of the following animals is not a mammal?*
>
> *A) Pig*
>
> *B) Shrew*
>
> *C) Whale*
>
> *D) Lizard*

The long preamble to the question is actually a distraction, which might cause you to miss that the question is actually asking you for a negative example, i.e. which of the examples is *not* a mammal. A careless reader would miss that and choose the first answer that seems right, which would be "A) Pig".

Tricky examiners might even make the other two wrong answers unfamiliar. For example, not many people may know that a shrew is also a mammal, thus mentally reinforcing "A) Pig" as the correct answer in the careless reader's mind.

Take the time to read the question carefully, reading every single word. Words like "not" or "except" can really trip you up if you miss them.

Use a pen to guide your eyes to help you focus. When you read the question, try to avoid immediately thinking of the answer. Our minds have a tendency to jump to conclusions. This blinds us to what is actually on the paper. Resist this temptation; keep your mind open and alert.

Answer the question thoroughly

Successful students thoroughly answer each question in a test. Even for multiple choice questions, they write down the working or reasoning behind each choice to facilitate checking later. For more complicated problems (especially in mathematics), they write down step-by-step solutions to make it easier for graders to give them partial credit if they make a mistake, and to make it easier for themselves to spot careless mistakes later.

Check your work if you have time

Careless or overconfident students leave out intervening steps in solving a problem (i.e. they jump straight to the answer), do not bother to check their work, and as a result lose precious points needlessly. You do not need to check your work after each question – you can do so after you have finished the exam.

Never leave an exam early. Some students like to leave an exam early to "show off" how smart they are ("this test was so easy I could do it in half the allotted time!"). Some students leave early because they give up. Don't be complacent and don't give up!

If you are done going through all the questions, do not waste precious time by leaving or sleeping. Spend it checking your work. It will be the last chance you have to do so.

The only time I have ever left an exam early was after checking through it thoroughly *twice*. Sometimes there really is too much time allotted for an exam, but those times are few and far between. If you have extra time, go through every single question and check your work. Go through each step in solving the problem again to see if you have made any careless mistakes. Then do it again.

Chapter Summary

✎ Attempt every question

✎ Read the question carefully

✎ Answer the question thoroughly

✎ Check your work if you have time

A Caveat On Languages

Before we move on to Part 2 where I share with you a system to optimally prepare for an exam, I'd like to say that the one subject this system doesn't work very well for is language exams, especially ones that are not content-based (e.g. memorizing a bunch of vocabulary words) but which test your fluency (e.g. in essays or oral exams).

Unfortunately I've learnt the hard way that building fluency in a language is a long-term process and cannot be crammed. You need daily, continuous effort to become good at it.

The classroom is not the best place to learn a language. Instead, an immersion program where you are surrounded by native speakers of the language and the cultural context (music, television, newspapers, art, literature, history) is the most effective way. If you want to develop proficiency in speaking, don't be shy. Keep using the language whenever and wherever you can.

Getting motivated

It helps to have a motivation to learn a language. I studied the Chinese language for twelve years but never spoke it outside of the classroom. The only contact I had with Chinese was through some television programs and music, which came in handy during karaoke sessions with friends. When I started work it became part of my job to invest in China (one of the largest and fastest growing economies in the world, amongst other things) and it became quite clear that I would need to use the language in my job to conduct meetings with company management. There is nothing like necessity to get you talking. Now I have a functional grasp of the language, but boy I sure wish I had paid more attention in class and used the language much more (ordering Chinese food doesn't count).

Note to the young: for the next few decades the global economy will be dominated by the rise of China, so learn the language and learn it well. Trust me – you will benefit tremendously from it.

I know another guy who was such a big fan of Japanese music, television drama serials and girls that he taught himself how to read and speak the language fluently. He even met a Japanese girl online and they started dating. She then moved to Singapore and they eventually got married. Talk about motivation! I spent five years learning Japanese in the classroom but I can hardly speak, read or write it. The difference is motivation.

Developing your proficiency

If you want to be able to write well, you have to first read a lot of quality material. Read up on subjects you are interested in; whether it's fiction or non-fiction doesn't matter. Even comic books are fine – just start reading.

Work on your pronunciation by listening to the radio or to newscasters. For English, I used to listen to BBC (British Broadcasting Corporation) radio in the morning during breakfast. Listen to the words newscasters use and how they pronounce every word. Try imitating them. Look I'm not saying you have to speak like an uppity snob. It's fine to use slang or speak stylishly sloppy when you're hanging out with your friends, but if you can't speak the language properly during crunch times (such as during presentations or interviews), then you can't call yourself proficient.

True proficiency in a language is one of those things that takes months and years to develop, and which requires continuous effort to improve. Sounds tiring, I know, but work on it. This may be one of the most useful and important things you learn, and is the foundation for effective communication.

Chapter Summary

✎ Building fluency in a language is a long-term process and requires continuous effort

✎ To write well, read quality material

✎ Work on your pronunciation by listening to the radio or to newscasters and imitating them

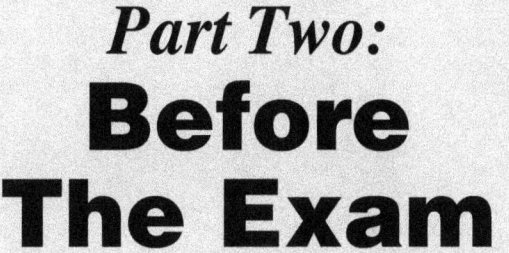

Part Two:
Before
The Exam

Brief Contents

Step One:
Know Your Enemy
(Find out the basics)

Preparing well for the exam is the key to getting great grades. There are four critical steps to take to be confidently prepared.

The first step is to know your enemy (i.e. the exam). This seems obvious, but you'd be surprised how many people do not know the basic details about the test they are about to take.

> *"If you know your enemy and you know yourself,*
> *you will not be imperilled in a hundred battles."*
> *— Sun Tzu (c. 6th century BC),*
> *author of The Art of War*

The basic questions to ask include:
When is the exam?

On what date and at what time will the exam be held? With this information you can calculate how much time you have left to prepare. Also, how long will the exam last?

Where will it be held?

If the location is somewhere you are unfamiliar with, it is worthwhile to make a trip down to the exam site and orientate yourself with the area, noting things like where the exam hall is and how long it takes you to get there. This is to prevent getting lost and arriving late for the exam.

What type of questions will appear on the exam?

Will the test consist of MCQs (multiple choice questions), short response questions, structured response questions (a passage followed by questions on it), or essay questions? Or a mix of those? If so, what is the mix? The type of questions that appear on a test will affect the way you prepare for it.

What subject material will be tested?

Find out exactly what topics will be appearing on the exam. You do not want to waste time studying for topics that will not appear, or miss topics that do. For example, some final exams do not test topics that were covered in a previous mid-term exam while some do.

What is important?

Which topics are critical and must be mastered because they will appear on the exam and comprise a large percentage of the marks? You find this out by paying attention in class and picking up cues from the teacher. They might say things like "pay particular attention to this topic" or "make sure you know how to do this". The top students then focus on the important material first to ensure they have nailed it before moving on to the less important stuff.

Chapter Summary

Make sure you can answer the following when you are preparing for an exam:

✎ When is the exam?

✎ Where will it be held?

✎ What type of questions will appear on the exam?

✎ What subject material will be tested?

✎ What is important?

Step Two: Plan Your Offence Strategy (Create the master plan)

Now that you know the "enemy" you are facing, it is time to plan your offence strategy.

Gather your resources

First gather all useful and relevant exam material, including textbooks, workbooks, guidebooks, handouts, homework, notes, and previous tests. Putting them all together in one pile will give you a good visual estimate of how much you have to do. Do this right at the beginning, because once you start preparing for the exam you do not want to waste any time scrounging around for other necessary resources.

Plan your time

Proper time planning is critical. It is the key to getting maximum results from minimum effort. To plan your time effectively:

➺ List out all topics in all subjects you will be tested on.

➺ Estimate how much time you need to cover an average topic, then double that estimate. You always take longer than you think – what I call the "Two Times Rule".

➺ Assign a specific date and time to every topic you

have to cover, in forty-five minute to one-hour chunks. For example, if you estimate you need two hours to complete the topic "The Properties of Matter", split it into two parts of one hour each.

➼ Remember to schedule brief breaks (from five to fifteen minutes each) between study sessions and to include the occasional longer break (thirty minutes to an hour) to exercise, read your email, de-stress on a computer game or chat with a friend. This prevents your brain from getting "burnt out", which then affects your absorption of the material.

The three times through system

When you study, your goal is to cover the material so thoroughly you are confident that no matter what questions appear on the exam, you will be able to answer them. And if you can't, nobody else who has studied the same material can. The keyword here is *confidence*. And one of the best ways to build that confidence is to go through the material multiple times, each time focusing more and more on the complex parts.

Ideally, you would have enough time to cover your material at least thrice. Your first run through is to give you a good feel for it and to build your understanding of the subject matter. Your second run through allows you to focus on the important points and commit them to memory. Your third run through is to review the material, ensuring you have not missed or forgotten anything, and to "lock in" that knowledge.

The first run through will take the most time as you are likely to be rusty with the material. The second run through will take less time, as you start to zoom in on areas you need to focus on – the more difficult, complex or meaty parts. The third run through should take the least time as you are just cementing in knowledge you already have (but may have some difficulty recalling in totality). Roughly speaking, the first run through will take twice as long as the second run through and four times as long as the third run through.

Don't forget to also budget time for doing practice tests. For example, if you have one month left to the exam, plan to do the first run through in two weeks, second run through in one week, and the third run through and practice tests in the last one.

The three times through system requires you to start preparing for the exam fairly early, and it does take time. But it is an efficient system (the second and third runs through will take much less time but will be very effective in helping you remember the material), and if you are willing to put the effort in to do it, will be tremendously rewarding.

Chapter Summary

✎ Gather all useful and relevant material for the exam

✎ Plan your preparation by listing out all subjects, estimating how much time you need to cover each, and assigning a date and time to study it

✎ Go through the material at least three times

Plan Your Offence Strategy

Step Three: Attack! (The daily routine)

Now that you've familiarized yourself with the details of the exam and have planned your strategy of attack, it is time to get down to the thrust and parry of the battle.

Take a question-oriented approach

When you begin studying, take a question-oriented approach. This involves asking questions about the material from every possible angle. Collect all the past year questions you can get your hands on, look in textbooks for end-of-chapter review questions, and brainstorm some of your own.

One thing you'll notice when compiling questions from different sources is the great degree of overlap in the kinds of questions that can be asked about any topic. That's where your confidence for taking the exam will come from, as you know that the mass of questions coming out on the test will be familiar to you. And if you prepared well, you'll even be able to tackle the occasional trick question or two.

Next, find the answers to these questions. If you come up with questions before you do your runs through the subject, you will subconsciously focus your mind to find the answers. Your study time will be more purposeful and productive because your mind has a goal.

Ensure the answers you prepare are accurate and

comprehensive. You are aiming to get full marks if the exact same question appears in the exam, which will give you a lot of leeway to screw up and make careless mistakes elsewhere, and takes pressure off you. You want to build your confidence to the point where you feel that no matter what, you will do well (at least on a relative basis).

Make your own notes

One of the most helpful ways to ensure the material sticks is to make your own notes. Only include key words and essential points, and use short forms you are familiar with. Feel free to use arrows and diagrams and any other shortcut that is useful and understandable to you – you are making the notes for your own use, so don't worry about anyone else finding them illegible.

Condense as much as you can. Summarize the information and only write down important details. Below you will find a table of common short forms to help you condense your notes.

Common Abbreviations For Note Taking

Word	Short form
against/versus	vs
and	&
approximately	≈
because	b/c
billions	b
change	Δ
decrease	↓
equals	=
especially	esp
for example	e.g.
government	govt
increase	↑
least	<<
less than	<
maximum	max
millions	m
minimum	min
money/cost/price	$
more than	>
most	>>
not equal	≠
number	#
page	p
parallel	//
percent	%
plus	+
results in/leads to	=>
that is	i.e.
thousands	k
with	w/
without	w/o
year	yr

I find putting pen to paper not only forces you to be disciplined about actually understanding the material and then stripping it to the bare essentials, but also helps you remember and recall the material as you involve another sense (touch) by writing things down.

Summarise your notes to one sheet of paper

Depending on how much material you have to cover you may end up with many pages of notes, but the goal is to summarise the entire subject material into one sheet of paper. This will be your eagle eye view of the exam material.

Once you have condensed the entire syllabus onto one sheet of paper, test yourself to see if you can expand it back out. Talk yourself through the whole process. If you can thoroughly explain a concept to someone else without referring to your notes, you know you really know your stuff.

Beef up your memory and study skills

There is much to learn about using your memory, developing good study strategies, and tools to optimise your learning efforts. I've excerpted some memory tips for you here from *The Student's Guide to Life*, but it would take a whole other book (or two) to cover these. Mastering these techniques will allow you to become more efficient with your studying.

Memory Tips For Optimum Recall

✳ **Make extensive use of memory aids (such as mnemonic devices).** There are memory tricks you can use to help you remember and (just as importantly) recall the information you need. For example, in *The Student's Guide to Life* I used the acronym ABCD to help you remember the four traits mature people possess (according to Dr. M. Scott Peck), namely that they i) **A**ccept responsibility for their lives ii) **B**alance the different parts of their lives iii) **C**onsciously live and iv) **D**elay gratification. You can find out more about using mnemonic devices at http://en.wikipedia.org/wiki/Mnemonic

✳ **Use flashcards.** For languages or subjects with a lot of jargon, make use of flashcards to help jog your recall. You can create flashcards for free at this site: http://www.flashcardexchange.com

✳ **Chunk things together.** It's hard to recall long lists of information. To make it easier to remember long lists, break the list into small and manageable groups, or "chunks".

✳ **Involve as many senses as you can.** For example, if you are trying to remember the Water Cycle, visualise the evaporation of water molecules from a body of water. See them rising through the air. Feel their increasing density as the temperature drops. See how they condense into clouds when they cannot remain as vapour anymore. Imagine you are flying through a fluffy cloud, which has been growing until it gets too heavy and the water droplets start to precipitate and fall back to the earth. Smell the rain, see the lightning from the storm and hear the roaring thunder. If it's like a scene from a movie, you'll find it hard to forget. If you want, make the images naughty or shocking. Too outrageous for you? Great, you'll remember it better.

One book I recommend is *What Smart Students Know* by Adam Robinson. Adam, an award winning school teacher in the United States, teaches you how to learn efficiently. For a comprehensive book on study techniques check out *How to Study* by Ron Fry. Ron covers topics such as note-taking, time management, reading and memory skills, and library research techniques.

Make sure you practise answering questions

Like I said in the first part of this book, there is a difference between studying for an exam and training for it. You do well in an exam by answering questions correctly, so that is what you should be practising. Find as many practice tests and questions you can (preferably with model answers you can check to gauge how much you know and save you time), then do them.

Chapter Summary

✎ Take a question-oriented approach to studying the material

✎ Prepare accurate and comprehensive answers to these questions

✎ Make your own condensed notes

✎ Summarise your notes to one sheet of paper and be able to expand it back out

✎ Beef up your memory and study skills

✎ Practise answering questions

Step Four:
On The Eve Of The Final Battle (The night before the exam)

You've studied the enemy, planned your attack, fought the good fight, and now you are at the eve of the final cataclysmic battle. Okay, maybe that's a little melodramatic. It's just an exam, after all. There are many scarier and tougher things in life. But it's not easy, so never underestimate your enemy. Be prepared.

Pack your bag properly

It is better to pack your bag the night before the exam rather than rush on the morning itself, when you will be nervous and might forget to bring a critical piece of stationery.

When you pack your bag, make sure you prepare a backup set of everything you need, including spare pens, pencils, and a calculator (or at least a battery) if necessary. While you might not think your brand new pen or newly-sharpened pencil will conk out on you during the exam, freak accidents have and will happen. More importantly, knowing you have a spare will help to calm your nerves and add to your feeling of preparedness (remember mind like water?).

If you have multiple exams during the day, don't forget

to pack food and water. I've found items such as energy or chocolate bars, and fruits such as bananas to be useful in keeping your energy level up. I usually also pack some sugar-free sweets as I find sucking on one helps me concentrate during the exam.

Here's a tip: get high quality stationery as they not only help you write faster, but also look better, which helps in exams where impression marking plays a part. Gel pens with a smooth ink flow can really speed up your writing during essay exams. Mechanical pencils save you time as you don't have to sharpen them, but don't forget to bring some spare lead refills.

Do a quick run through of the most important points

Remember that one-page summary you prepared as part of the process of condensing your notes down to the essential ideas? Use it to cement the key points in your mind, and see if you can expand those points out to the secondary ideas and the supporting details without referring to any materials. If you can, you're set. If you can't, you know where to focus those last few precious hours before you sleep.

Get a good night's rest

Relax, you have done all you can to prepare for this exam. Rest well the night before – the extra benefit you get from an hour's more sleep is much greater than doing an extra hour of studying. There is no point pulling an all-nighter. It will cost you the concentration and mental agility you need to ace the exam.

I know this is very unlikely, but thanks to Murphy's Law (where everything that can go wrong will, and usually at the worst time), if you usually only use one alarm clock it may fail you on that all-important exam morning. To minimize this possibility (or at least to reassure your worried mind that this could happen), set two alarm clocks. Then tuck yourself into bed, and start thinking about woolly sheep or anything other than your exam.

Chapter Summary

✎ Pack your bag the night before

✎ Do a quick run through of the most important points before you sleep

✎ Get a good night's rest

Part Three:

The Day Of
The Exam

Brief Contents

The Morning Of The Exam

I hope you've gotten a good night's rest, because this is it. Today you prove whether you are made of steel or cotton.

Eat a nutritious breakfast. Double check that all your stationery and anything you need for the exam is packed in your bag.

Aim to arrive fifteen to thirty minutes early for the exam, so you have ample time to familiarize yourself with the environment and relax. There is nothing more nerve-wracking than arriving late for an exam. Trust me, I've been there.

Chapter Summary

✎ Eat a nutritious breakfast

✎ Check your stationery and other supplies before you leave for the exam

✎ Arrive fifteen to thirty minutes early

Right Before The Exam

So you're sitting at your desk, nervously wringing your hands and waiting for the exam to start. Develop a ritual to mentally prepare yourself for the exam. Start with your breathing. Take slow, deep breaths to calm down and relax. If you believe in God, say a prayer. I never pray for good grades, but for a clear head, peace of mind, and the opportunity to demonstrate what I have learnt.

Lay your stationery neatly on the table, ensuring everything is out of the way but within easy reach when you need it. For time management purposes, I find it helps to take my watch off and prop it on the table like a little clock. Sometimes you get so caught up in the exam you forget the time, so it helps to have the watch right in front of you to remind you.

Chapter Summary

✎ Take slow, deep breaths to calm down and relax

✎ Lay your stationery neatly on the table before the exam begins

When The Exam Begins

Usually, when you are handed the test paper you have to wait till everyone gets a copy before you can begin. Use this time to read the instructions, and pay attention to guidelines such as where you should write your answers (e.g. on the exam paper itself or on a separate answer sheet), the different sections of the paper, and the total time allocated. Sometimes a critical instruction on the cover could be missed (e.g. "choose three out of five questions to answer") that will cause you lots of grief if you miss it.

Once the teacher/invigilator says "you may begin", resist the temptation to jump in and start answering questions. Instead, flip through every page of the exam and skim the questions, keeping an eye out for things like:

➤ Missing pages (i.e. check if the page numbers tally)

➤ The different topics tested and the marks allocated to each topic

➤ Which questions look easy to you and which look difficult

This should take a minute or two at most. The point is to get a feel for the entire exam, so you can keep the big picture in mind and not get lost in the details.

Before you start the most important thing is to plan your time – mentally allocate time to each section and question based on how many points they are worth.

Examples Of Time Allocation

Example #1

Exam type	: Multiple Choice Questions (MCQ)
Number of questions	: 30
Points	: 2 per question for a total of 60
Time	: 1 hour (or 1 minute per point)
Question allocation	: 2 minutes per question

Example #2

Exam type	: MCQ + Short response
Number of questions	: 10 MCQs + 5 short response
Points	: 1 per MCQ and 2 per short response for a total of 20
Time	: 40 minutes (or 2 minutes per point)
Question allocation	: 2 minutes per MCQ and 4 minutes per short response
Section allocation	: 20 minutes for MCQs and 20 minutes for short response

Example #3

Exam type	: MCQ + Short response + Essay

Number of questions :	20 MCQs + 5 short response + 1 essay
Points :	1 per MCQ, 2 per short response, and 10 for the essay for a total of 40
Time :	1 hour 20 minutes (or 2 minutes per point)
Question allocation :	2 minutes per MCQ, 4 minutes per short response, and 20 minutes for the essay
Section allocation :	40 minutes for MCQs, 20 minutes for short response, and 20 minutes for the essay

Keeping track of your allocated time will ensure you have enough time to make a decent attempt at each question. Good time management is essential – you do not want to be in a situation where the time has run out and you have left easy questions blank, thus wasting precious points.

The per question time allocation gives you a mental guide of roughly how long you should spend on each question, but there's no need to compulsively keep track of how much time you are spending on every single question.

That's where the section time allocation comes in. When you're roughly halfway through the section, you can check how much time you've used and whether you need to speed up to meet the time allocated for the section. For instance in Example #2 above if you're halfway through the MCQ section and you notice that fifteen minutes have already passed, then you know you need to speed up as you only have five minutes to finish the section.

These time allocations are a guideline to keep you on track to finish the exam, but if you really need a few extra minutes to finish a section go ahead. Just remember you have to make that time up by working quicker on the next section.

You will definitely do better on the exam by attempting every question and skipping a few tough questions, versus trying to solve a few difficult questions and leaving half the exam blank. Agree?

Get used to doing this mental time allocation every time you take an exam. Once you're used to it, it'll take the better part of ten seconds to do. And I guarantee it'll be the most rewarding ten seconds you ever spent on an exam.

Once you've done your time allocation, dive in! There are at least three different strategies on how you should "attack" the exam:

1. Start from the front and work your way through
2. Do all the easy questions first and leave the hard ones last
3. Answer the hard questions first and leave the easy questions last

The advantage of the first approach ("front to back straight through") is that it is simple. You don't have to go through the exam and figure out which questions are hard or easy. You just start from the first question and work your way through to the last one.

The advantage of the second approach ("easy first/hard last") is it helps you knock off the easy points first. A point scored on an easy question is worth the same as a point scored on a difficult one, so why not spend most of your time maximizing your marks on the easy ones? Then when you have time left over, you can go back and tackle the hard ones.

The advantage of the third approach ("hard first/easy last") is that you can tackle the hardest questions at the beginning when your mind is fresh, and once you're done with those, you will feel more confident about the rest of the exam as they're all easy questions.

Choose the approach that works best for you. For me, I've always used the simple approach of working from front to back, as I find it takes too much time to figure out which are the easy or hard questions on the test, time which I might as well spend just attempting the question. The caveat is that I keep a close watch on the time I am spending on each question. If the question takes too long to answer (most likely because it is difficult), I will move on to the next one and only go back when I am done with the rest of the exam.

Actually answer the question

Many careless mistakes are made because students do not read questions carefully. When I say carefully I mean reading *every single word.* It is a useful practice to underline keywords – action verbs and important information. Action verbs are a guide on what the examiner wants from you.

For complicated mathematics, science or logic questions, I find it useful to draw a diagram to clarify the relationships between things in a question.

You can read more tips and tricks to answering different types of questions in "Part 5 – Specific Applications".

Keep going, don't stop!

Keep the momentum going. If you get stuck on a question and have no idea how to answer it, move on! Tell yourself it doesn't matter, because you have prepared well for this exam and you should know enough to answer the rest of the questions and get a good grade despite flubbing a few.

Always keep track of the time you are spending on each question (if there are only a few big questions) and/or each section (if there are many questions split up by sections.) Make it a habit to look at your watch intermittently throughout the exam. Good time management is the key to getting good grades.

Chapter Summary

✎ Read the instructions carefully

✎ When time begins, flip through every page of the exam and skim the questions

✎ Allocate time to each section and question based on how many points they are worth

✎ Read and answer the questions carefully

✎ Keep going, don't stop!

✎ Keep track of the time you are spending on each section

Near The End Of The Exam

If you managed your time well, you will finish before you run out of time. Depending on how well you had prepared and the difficulty of the exam, there may be some questions half-completed or barely attempted, but instead of wasting time on those you moved on (which is the right thing to do).

Check your answers

If you have time remaining, do not waste it by sleeping or leaving the exam early. Never leave early unless you've checked for mistakes at least twice over. Spend it either attempting questions you could not answer the first time round, or if there are none of those, by checking your answers.

To check your answers, read through each question carefully again, and go through your answer step-by-step, checking each and every part. Do not assume you will not make any careless mistakes just because the question is easy.

There may be questions whose answers you are unsure about. Only change the answer if you have a good reason to, such as: you made a careless mistake, misread the question, or remembered new information you hadn't thought of before. If not, go with your first answer.

Use your time wisely, because before you know it you'll hear "time's up!"

Chapter Summary

If you have extra time:

- ✎ Attempt questions you skipped
- ✎ Check your answers at least twice through

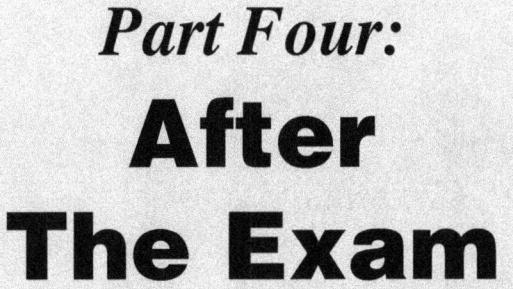

Part Four:
After
The Exam

Brief Contents

Right After The Exam

Hand in your paper, get out of the classroom and breathe some fresh air. There's no point discussing the paper with your classmates, as you'll only fret about the questions you didn't answer correctly. What's the point of wasting time and giving yourself a downer when there's absolutely nothing you can do about it?

However you actually did, you know the results are much better than if you had not properly prepared. Give yourself a pat on the back, then go relax and reward yourself.

Chapter Summary

After the exam:

✎ Don't waste time discussing answers with others

✎ Go relax and reward yourself

Post-Mortem (When you get your results back)

Sometimes teachers take a day or two to grade tests, sometimes weeks, but it always feels like a long time. I still remember the sharp moment of anxiety I felt when graded tests were distributed.

A returned test is an opportunity for you to conduct a post-mortem (an analysis of an event after it is over) to figure out where you lost points and areas to improve on the next time round.

For questions you lost points on, was it because:

You made a careless mistake

Did you make a wrong calculation? Did you misread the question? Did you shade the wrong circle or write the wrong answer?

We're only human and we make mistakes. However, successful students are able to focus and minimize careless mistakes. If you made a lot of careless mistakes, you likely have a problem with focusing.

Just as the body needs exercise to build strength and stamina, you brain needs training to build focus. Learn how to pay active attention to material in front of you – when your mind wanders, force it to return to the task. This is a tiring thing to do, but over time as you keep refocusing your attention, your mental "muscles" will be strengthened.

You didn't know the answer

Was the material tested within the assigned syllabus? If not, don't take it too hard. Unless you did some sort of extra reading outside of your school materials (which I highly recommend if you are interested in the subject matter), there was no way you could know the answer.

If the question tested material within the syllabus, it means you need to work harder on your preparation plan for the next test. Perhaps you have to allocate more time to adequately cover the material, or to work on your study and memory skills.

Sometimes due to time constraints you are forced to skip certain topics that are too hard or time consuming to get the most bang for your studying buck. In that instance it's the right thing to do. But plan to start earlier for the next test.

You blanked out because you were nervous

Some people are more nervous about taking tests than others. Hey, there's no doubt it's a stressful event. You've got time pressure, peer pressure, parental pressure, a teacher breathing down your neck, and oh by the way, your entire future rests on those two hours (or so it seems).

If you never exercise and decided to run a marathon

you'd not only be unable to complete it but would also hurt yourself. In the same way, you have to build up your "exam muscles" to feel confident about tackling a test. The key is to have adequate preparation and good time management.

For each test you take aim to do a little better – build your confidence bit by bit. If you approach each test seriously and do what I outline in this book, I promise in (at most) a couple years time you won't even remember you had a problem taking tests.

You didn't attempt the question

I've said earlier that you should always attempt every question (unless there are penalties for wrong answers), even if you have no idea how to go about it. Just put down some ideas you think are relevant, or even describe briefly how you would answer the question if you had the right information. A point is a point, and there's no shame in getting a sympathy point.

So the only reasons for not attempting a question are if you ran out of time or just missed the question completely out of carelessness. Either way, both are symptoms of poor exam time management.

If you manage your time properly during an exam, you should never have unanswered questions at the end of an exam. It is better to leave a tough question half-answered and move on to the next one then to have one comprehensively answered question and a bunch of blank ones.

In Economics there is a Law of Diminishing Returns which states that beyond a certain point each additional unit of input yields less and less output. In the test-taking context each additional minute you spend on a question is worth fewer and fewer additional points. Spending five minutes on a question might get you 80% of the points. Spending another five minutes will only get you at most another 10-20% of the points. It is better to spend that second five minutes working on another question to get 80% of the points there.

If you missed a question due to carelessness (e.g. you didn't even see it), that means you probably: 1) Didn't do a quick flip through of the test at the beginning (which you should have done in order to estimate how much time you could spend on each question) and/or 2) Didn't leave enough time at the end to check your work.

I can't stress this point often enough: Good time management before and during the exam is the key to schooling success.

Chapter Summary

✎ Do a post-mortem after the exam to figure out where you went wrong and how you can do better next time

Part Five:
Specific Applications

Brief Contents

Multiple Choice Questions

Multiple Choice Questions (MCQs) often appear in tests as they are easy to grade and an efficient way to evaluate your mastery of a large body of knowledge. Here is my system for scoring in MCQ exams:

- Read the question carefully and underline key words (watch out for tricky words such as "not", "always", "never")

- Go through *all* the answers and eliminate those you know are wrong (don't just pick the first answer you think is right)

- After the process of elimination, if you have only one answer left, choose that as the right answer

- If there are multiple answers left and you cannot eliminate anymore after working out the question, guess (unless there is a penalty for a wrong answer)

- If two answers are very similar (e.g. two numbers that differ only slightly, or two shapes that look alike), it is likely that one of them is the right answer

- If in doubt over the meaning of the question, ask a teacher and/or go with the more obvious explanation. Do not read too much into the question

To improve your performance on MCQ tests, do the following during your preparation:

➤ Focus on the details. MCQs tend to test you on specific pieces of information that you would miss if you only focused on the big picture concepts.

➤ Memorize definitions of key terms. As the options for MCQs tend to be very close to each other to confuse you, memorizing definitions will help you pick the answer that is exactly right.

➤ Understand multiple-step processes and event sequences. Often you will see MCQs (especially in science exams) that require you to understand and place the steps of a process in the correct order.

Short Answer Questions

For short answer questions you are asked a question and are given a small space (from one to a couple of lines) to answer it.

Short answer questions are usually looking for a specific answer, so be clear, concise, and make sure you include key jargon (technical terms). Look at the number of marks given as a guide to how many answers you need to give.

Essay Questions

In essay tests examiners are determining the extent to which candidates are able to:

- Communicate clearly and effectively
- Write fluently and grammatically
- Plan, organise and write coherently

The following approach is more applicable for argumentative essays (as opposed to creative or free writing questions), but some of the steps are applicable to both.

Read the question carefully

Underline any important information and action verbs – find out exactly what the question is asking of you. The table below contains the most commonly used action verbs in essay questions and what you should do.

Common Action Verbs For Essay Tests

Action verb	Meaning
Analyse	Break into parts and logically discuss each part
Compare	Explain similarities and differences between two or more items
Contrast	Distinguish between items by focusing on differences
Criticise	Evaluate the positive and negative aspects of what is being discussed
Define	State accurate meaning
Describe	Give information that paints a complete picture
Discuss	Examine in a comprehensive way, usually by connecting ideas to examples
List	Specify appropriate items in the form of a list
Evaluate	Give your opinion about the value or correctness of something, usually by weighing positive and negative effects, and justifying your conclusion
Explain	Make clear the meaning of something, often by making analogies or giving examples
Illustrate	Supply examples
Outline	Present the main ideas and sub-ideas in a clear structure
State	Explain clearly and concisely
Summarise	Provide the important ideas in brief

Outline your answer

Having a proper structure to your essay is the key to scoring well. Every argumentative essay should have the following:

A. Introduction

B. Arguments/counter-arguments (if a balanced viewpoint is required) supported by examples

C. Conclusion

The introduction and conclusion of your essay are crucial. In both of these paragraphs clearly show you are answering the question.

To improve your performance on essay tests, ensure you know the main points and ideas, and the supporting details of each topic. You can go one step further and prepare essay outlines for different topics with the key points in summary form.

Other tips to tackle the essay test:

➤ Plan your time. Assign a time limit to writing each part of your essay

➤ Keep to the point. Don't pad your essays with lots of meaningless fluff. Use clear, short sentences

➤ If time runs out, write your answer in point form. This is where making a plan in the beginning will prove useful

➤ Read through the essay afterwards to correct grammar and spelling mistakes

Remember: Impression marking is important. You must write legibly and neatly; use a pen with dark ink to improve readability.

Your essay should have a logical flow of ideas, which is achieved by planning the structure at the beginning. You should also clearly indicate your main points and make them easy to spot (I've even gone to the extent of underlining them sometimes).

The whole point is to make it as painless as possible for your examiner to understand your arguments and to award you marks. Put yourself in his or her shoes – imagine the examiner trying to rush through grading a stack of fifty essays before watching a movie with the spouse and kids. Make his or her life as easy as possible and don't do anything annoying!

The best book I know to master the art of clear and concise writing (and it's short too!) is *The Elements of Style* by William Strunk and E. B. White (White is also author of *Charlotte's Web*). Get a copy and read it often.

Mathematics Questions

Solving tough mathematics problems requires a systematic approach:

1. What do I know?

- ➺ Underline information given in the problem
- ➺ Express this information in mathematical symbols, if possible

2. What do I want?

- ➺ Figure out what the problem is asking you to find (i.e. the goal), circling key words if necessary

3. What can I do?

- ➺ Write down any relevant formulas
- ➺ Try manipulating and combining the given information to see if you can get closer to the goal
- ➺ Do one step at a time
- ➺ Draw a diagram to clarify the relationship between people or things
- ➺ Look for a pattern
- ➺ Simplify the problem (try substituting simple numbers)
- ➺ Work backwards
- ➺ If you really have no idea, guess and see if it works (i.e. trial and error)

4. Does it make sense?

➤➤ Look at the original question and look at your answer again – does it feel right?

➤➤ Do you have the correct units (cm, kg, etc.)?

To reduce careless mistakes, practise estimating the answer mentally. For example:

> *If you divide an inheritance of $56,580 among 11 heirs, how much will each heir receive?*
> *A) $51.44*
> *B) $565.80*
> *C) $5,143.64*
> *D) $51,436.40*

If I ask you to choose the right answer without actually working it out, could you? Here's how to do it: estimate the answer mentally using simpler numbers, e.g. just divide $50,000 by 10. So you know the answer should be around $5,000 and you can select "C" as the correct answer without even doing any calculations.

By estimating answers mentally and not constantly relying on a calculator, you will gradually develop a feel for numbers that will help you work faster and more accurately.

In non-MCQ mathematics questions, don't forget to show every step of your working even if you're smart enough to skip a couple of steps. Sometimes examiners need to see the proper sequence of steps before they can award you full marks; sometimes if you make a careless mistake they will give you partial credit if you had shown the correct steps. So don't be lazy!

Reading Comprehension

Reading comprehension tests typically include a short essay followed by several questions that are based on it.

For reading comprehension questions, most people tend to start reading the passage before looking at the questions. Don't do that! Instead, read the questions *before* reading the passage. This will give you an idea of what information you are supposed to find and will make your reading of the passage more focused and efficient.

If you read the passage first, when you get to the questions you have to go back and reread the passage to locate the relevant information, unnecessarily wasting time. Instead, read the questions first, then when you read the passage underline any information you can use to answer the questions.

Read through the entire passage before answering questions as sometimes a complete answer to a question could come from multiple parts of the passage.

Open Book Tests

The temptation when taking an open book test is to study too little for it ("why bother when you can just find the answer in the textbook?"). That is a mistake. By under studying and leaving yourself unfamiliar with the material you will waste a large amount of time locating relevant information during the exam and not enough time actually answering the questions.

To do well in an open book test, you should still prepare a summary sheet with references to where you can find information. Use post-its to mark the location of important information in your books.

Do commit critical information to memory – the difficulty in open book tests is not in knowing the right answer but in successfully compiling the information into a coherent argument within a limited time.

Oral Examinations

Oral exams can be split into three types: reading, picture description and conversation tests. We shall look at how to ace each separately.

Reading exams

Some oral exams require you to read a passage out loud. To score in these you need to:

➦ Read with good pronunciation and clear articulation

➦ Read with the appropriate rhythm and stress on words (i.e. fluently)

➦ Read expressively with the appropriate variation of pitch and tone

Some tips to ace reading aloud tests:

➦ Articulate clearly. In our normal day-to-day conversations we tend to be quite lazy in articulating, but during a test you need to be conscientious about speaking properly. Pay particular attention to the ends of words (e.g. 'c', 's', 'd', 't' and 'n'). Try saying: "His account of the dreaded termination was fantastic."

➦ Pause for the appropriate amount of time when you see punctuation marks. In general you should pause for increasingly long periods of time in this order: commas(,), semicolons(;), colons(:) and full stops(.).

➤➤ Vary your pitch and loudness while reading the passage to emphasize and dramatize the important parts to increase interest for the listener.

Developing mastery of a language and sensitivity to its nuances takes time and effort. It helps to listen to news broadcasts to get the articulation and pronunciation right. In terms of learning how to vary your pitch and loudness, it might help to take drama classes.

Picture description exams

Some oral exams require you to look at a picture or photograph and discuss it intelligently, including being able to:

➤➤ Interpret and explain the situation in the picture with the use of supporting details

➤➤ Use appropriate vocabulary and sentence structures

➤➤ Develop ideas in a clear and coherent way

To score you should discuss the picture in a structured way:

1. First give an overview of the picture, e.g. "This is a picture of a busy road with towering blocks of public housing in the background."

2. Next delve into details of the people or surroundings, e.g. "In the foreground there is a middle-aged woman holding a young boy's hand, waiting to cross the road at the traffic light. The young boy is wearing a school

uniform and appears to be her son. There are a lot of cars, buses and trucks speeding by on one side of the road, and fewer on the other side."

3. Then explain why, when or how such a scene may happen, e.g. "Given the lighting and the one-sided traffic on the road, this scene is probably taking place during the morning rush hour. The mother appears to be taking her son to school while the commuters in the vehicles are rushing to work."

4. Finally add any interesting insights or observations you have about the significance of the scene, e.g. "This scene depicts the day-to-day life of ordinary people living in a suburban neighbourhood – parents taking their kids to school, adults heading to work, all in an orderly way and with proper observation of the traffic rules."

Conversation exams

Some oral exams require you to have a conversation with the examiner in response to prompts about a picture or passage, or questions he or she asks about general topics. To score in these:

➡ Express yourself clearly using appropriate vocabulary and sentence structure

➡ Respond accurately to the examiner's prompts and questions

➻ Engage the examiner with a personal response to the issues raised

The key thing examiners are looking for is your ability to carry out an interesting and smooth-flowing conversation.

When you are asked a question, reply in a full sentence and add on appropriate information. Instead of just answering "yes" or "no", you could say something like: "Yes, I think his actions were criminally irresponsible. He should have called for an ambulance right away instead of driving off and abandoning the old lady he knocked down."

Be friendly, confident and engaging. The candidate who will score well is one who does not need much prompting to share interesting and intelligent views, who speaks up confidently and clearly, and who seems personable and positive. And don't forget to smile when you greet the examiners!

Some Final Words

Congratulations! You made it to the end of this book. I hope what I have shared will help you succeed in school. But please be aware that the philosophy and system I espouse in this book are geared towards acing exams. They do not necessarily encourage a passion for learning or a desire to gain knowledge for its own sake. The focus of this book is to get you the best possible grades in the most efficient way, because exams are crucial in determining the future opportunities available to you.

But I fear you will be so focused on grades you become unwilling to spend time understanding what you are learning and its relevance to the real world, and thus unable to find pleasure in the process. Learning can and should be fun and meaningful.

One thing I cannot stress enough: Exams are important but are not everything. You should not let your sense of self-worth be determined by a score on a piece of paper. The whole point of this book is to help you master the game of testing to free up time and energy to do worthwhile things such as pursuing a hobby, learning things you are interested in, spending time with friends, or making somebody else's life better.

May your road ahead be filled with good grades, great friends, and tons of belly laughs.

Take care,
Andrew K.J. Tan

Appendix I:
Why do I have to go to school?

(This chapter is excerpted from **The Student's Guide to Life** *by Andrew K.J. Tan)*

I learnt the true value of my education at fifteen when I took a holiday job at a prestigious luxury hotel. Let me describe my job in greater detail. Guests checked into the hotel, and in doing whatever they do in hotel rooms they made use of both towels and bed sheets. When they checked out, the maids (not I) would gather the soiled linen and cart it off to a large central chute located in the back area of every floor. A five-star hotel might look grand, spotless and gleaming marble to you, but the back area where the staff work is often a slum.

Let's say the maids are cleaning rooms on the fifteenth floor. They stuff a bundle of linen into the chute, and this bundle hurtles downwards, accelerating according to the laws of gravity. Upon reaching the basement level, this bundle would pop out of the chute opening with a large WHOOMP and hurtle across an enclosed, windowless holding area, smashing into the opposite wall before falling onto the floor.

There I was in this stuffy, humid, lint-filled room, avoiding deadly cannonballs of linen while separating the mountain of towels and bed sheets into two carts. These were not your ordinary bed sheets and towels but the wet, stained, sticky, I-really-do-not-want-to-know-how-these-were-used type. Once these carts were full I would push them out of this room, down a hallway and load them onto a truck. Sounds like a dream job, doesn't it?

This was a daily-rated, low paying job with no chance of advancement whatsoever. Everyday I would line up at a counter to collect thirty dollars in cash for my ten hours of work. I worked there for a month.

After that experience, I felt a great desire to return to school, give my desk a kiss and study like I never did before. I felt then that the purpose of my education was to do so well I could sit in an air-conditioned office staring at a computer all day long for the rest of my life.

If you've ever worked at a job serving fast food or carrying crates of stuff around, you know the feeling of being trapped in an unrewarding, dead end job. People working in these jobs are often just trying to survive, to make enough money to put some food on the table for their families. They have neither the skills nor the education to get a better job and carve out a more comfortable existence for themselves.

Education is your key to socioeconomic mobility. Even if you come from a poor family, if you make the most of your education and pick up some useful skills and knowledge, you have the opportunity to work in a more rewarding career, both financially and in terms of your job satisfaction. There is a direct correlation between your level of education and how much money you will make in a job.

Everyday in school when you're facing the whiteboard or a textbook, don't think in terms of trying to pass an exam; think in terms of building a better life for yourself and your family in the future.

Why you should get the best education you possibly can

Do you know why you are going to school? Is it only because you are expected to? If you find you drag yourself to school every morning, and would rather count the number of cracks on the ceiling than pay attention to the lesson, you need to know the advantages of having an education:

- **You have more opportunities in life.** With more doors open, you have more choices in life. My freedom is important to me, and if I'm able to earn enough to not have to worry about my day-to-day survival, I can begin to explore the possibilities in life. Your education is also something you can always fall back on. As my mom says: "Your business can go bankrupt, your shares can fall to zero, but your education is something no one can take away from you."

- **It stretches your mind.** With education, you gain a greater understanding of the world around you – how things work, why things are the way they are. Both the breadth (in terms of the number of things you know) and the depth (in terms of how well you know these things) of your insight will expand.

➼ **For the love of learning and knowledge.** Learning, if based on your interests, is fun and could even be exhilarating.

➼ **As a step towards maximizing your potential.** Don't let your brain go to waste. Your ability is only limited by your imagination.

See the bigger picture. Going to school and "getting an education" is not about textbooks, worksheets, grades and exams. It is about changing the lens through which you see the world, fitting you with wings to aid you on your journey through it, and giving you the master key to the locked doors of opportunity.

Appendix II:
Six things parents can do
to help

1) Set up a study corner

If space allows, set aside a quiet corner of the home as an exclusive area for your kid to study and do his or her homework. Make sure it is far away from the TV, phone, and any other potential distractions. An exclusive study corner will help your kid to focus and concentrate on school work in his or her own space.

2) Establish a routine

Let's face it – very few kids like to study or do their homework. By setting up a routine, you can help boost your kid's learning productivity and also ensure regular studying, which will boost recall (and thus grades) during exams.

3) Make reading a habit for your kid

Reading regularly is key to developing your child's linguistic abilities and a trait of lifelong learners. Either fiction or non-fiction is fine. Be an example by setting up a reading time when both parent and child can read together.

4) Limit TV and computer time

Watching TV, surfing the web, playing computer games or chatting with friends are some of the biggest time sucks out there, and also a major source of distraction. Have an agreement with your kid that limits their time spent doing these things on a daily basis.

5) Persuade them to do their homework before playing

It's tough to do in practice, but help your kid learn how to delay gratification by making it a condition that they finish their homework before they are allowed to have recreational/personal time.

6) Encourage, not nag

Finally and most importantly, be a source of encouragement and not a source of annoyance/irritation to your kids. They need to know that you care before they'll listen to you. Praise them for putting in effort; console them when they fail. Inspire them to love learning and to achieve excellence by setting a personal example.

About the author

Andrew K. J. Tan was born and raised in Singapore, where he spent his first twenty years, before going on scholarship to Stanford University in Palo Alto, California. A top student and member of Phi Beta Kappa (the oldest American academic honours society), he earned a Bachelor in Economics (Distinction) along with a Master in Management Science and Engineering in four years.

While at Stanford he was selected to be head academic counsellor of a sixty-person dorm, and supervised a team of peer advisors. He also managed over forty tutors to provide subject tutoring for the entire undergraduate community.

At the age of twenty-four he became Site Director of the Stanford Asia Technology Initiative, where he helped set up the inaugural Global Entrepreneurship Conference in Singapore.

Andrew has written for *Teens Magazine* and is currently a fund manager at a global investment firm. He is also the author of *The Student's Guide to Life*. In his spare time he loves to read, sing and dream.

The Student's Guide to Life

Essential lessons on love, learning and success

"Gives great insight on the best ways to handle everyday tricky situations." - Seventeen

"A useful guide for anyone dealing with the young." - Lifestyle

"Andrew pours candid yet practical advice to teenagers of all ages." - Teenage

---

The Student's Guide to Life is a must-have guidebook for twelve to twenty-plus year olds.

Inside they will learn how to:
★ Deal with emotional and self-esteem issues
★ Interact in a healthy way with parents, siblings and teachers
★ Make new friends and build lifelong friendships
★ Handle romantic relationships
★ Excel in school without studying all the time
★ Set goals, manage their time and achieve their dreams

Students have a tough time; sometimes they need a bit of help to get through sticky situations. The Student's Guide to Life will help them thrive instead of just survive, using minimum effort to achieve maximum results.

Available at leading bookstores and online at www.aktive.com.sg

Student Entrepreneurship Program

**If you are a student in a
Singapore school, make some extra
allowance or raise funds
for a student group or charity
by signing up for this program.**

In this program you will learn and get to practise:

✱ Business Basics

✱ Creative Marketing

✱ Ethical Selling

✱ Customer Satisfaction

Interested? Find out more at www.aktive.com.sg